COLFAX
OCT 2018

INSECTS UP CLOSE

Crickets

by Patrick Perish

BLASTOFF! READERS

BELLWETHER MEDIA • MINNEAPOLIS, MN

Note to Librarians, Teachers, and Parents:

Blastoff! Readers are carefully developed by literacy experts and combine standards-based content with developmentally appropriate text.

Level 1 provides the most support through repetition of high-frequency words, light text, predictable sentence patterns, and strong visual support.

Level 2 offers early readers a bit more challenge through varied simple sentences, increased text load, and less repetition of high-frequency words.

Level 3 advances early-fluent readers toward fluency through increased text and concept load, less reliance on visuals, longer sentences, and more literary language.

Level 4 builds reading stamina by providing more text per page, increased use of punctuation, greater variation in sentence patterns, and increasingly challenging vocabulary.

Level 5 encourages children to move from "learning to read" to "reading to learn" by providing even more text, varied writing styles, and less familiar topics.

Whichever book is right for your reader, Blastoff! Readers are the perfect books to build confidence and encourage a love of reading that will last a lifetime!

This edition first published in 2019 by Bellwether Media, Inc.

No part of this publication may be reproduced in whole or in part without written permission of the publisher. For information regarding permission, write to Bellwether Media, Inc., Attention: Permissions Department, 6012 Blue Circle Drive, Minnetonka, MN 55343.

Library of Congress Cataloging-in-Publication Data

Names: Perish, Patrick, author.
Title: Crickets / by Patrick Perish.
Description: Minneapolis, MN : Bellwether Media, Inc., [2019] | Series: Blastoff! Readers: Insects Up Close | Includes bibliographical references and index.
Identifiers: LCCN 2017056257 (print) | LCCN 2017058891 (ebook) | ISBN 9781626178038 (hardcover : alk. paper) | ISBN 9781681035284 (ebook)
Subjects: LCSH: Crickets–Juvenile literature.
Classification: LCC QL508.G8 (ebook) | LCC QL508.G8 P47 2018 (print) | DDC 595.7/26–dc23
LC record available at https://lccn.loc.gov/2017056257

Editor: Christina Leaf   Designer: Tamara JM Peterson

Printed in the United States of America, North Mankato, MN

Table of Contents

What Are Crickets?

Crickets are insects with long legs. They chirp beautiful songs in the dark.

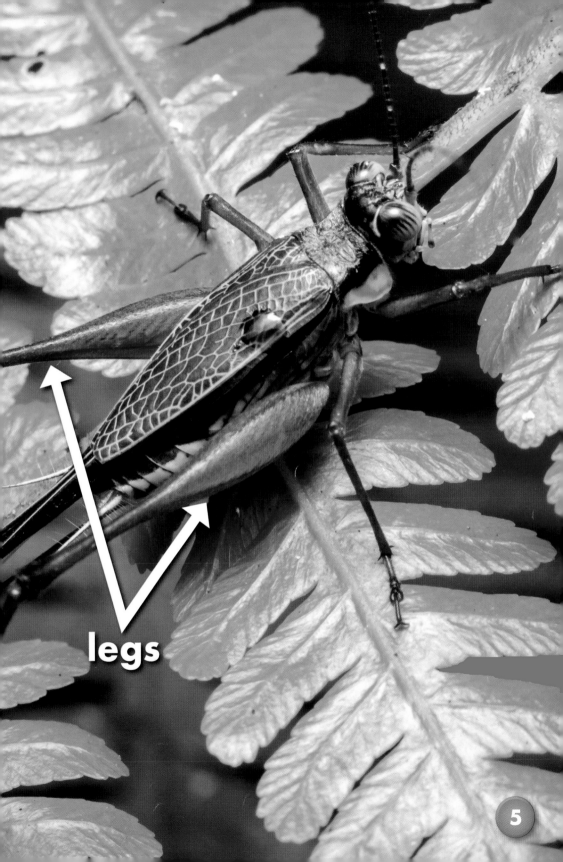

legs

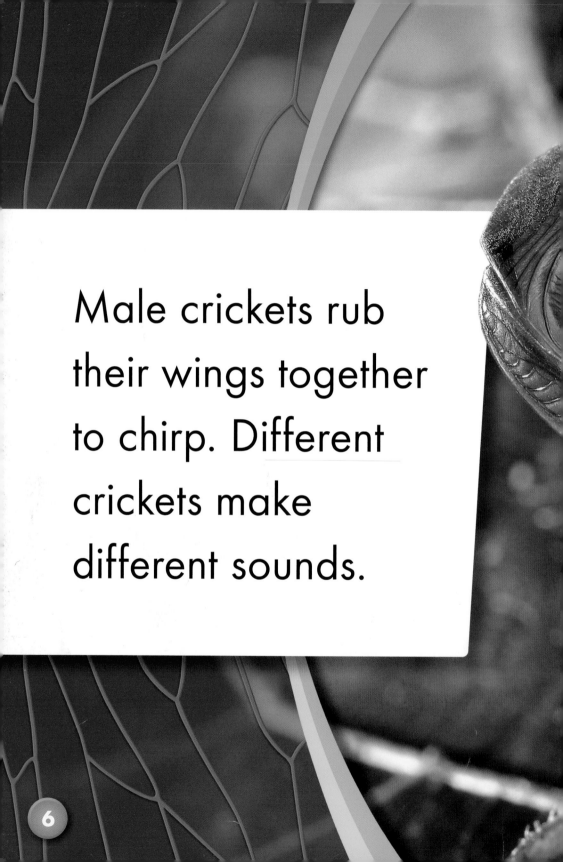

Male crickets rub their wings together to chirp. Different crickets make different sounds.

wings

Crickets have **eardrums** on their legs. Females listen for the males' songs.

ACTUAL SIZE:
field cricket

eardrum

9

Crickets can be black, brown, and green. Long **antennae** help them smell.

antennae

Life in the Grass

Crickets live in grassy fields and forests. They are most active at night.

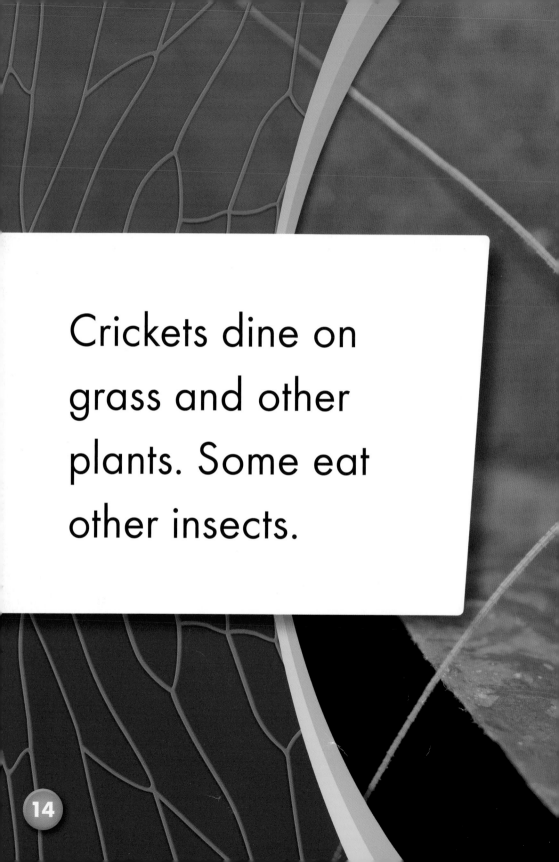

Crickets dine on grass and other plants. Some eat other insects.

FAVORITE FOOD:

grass

15

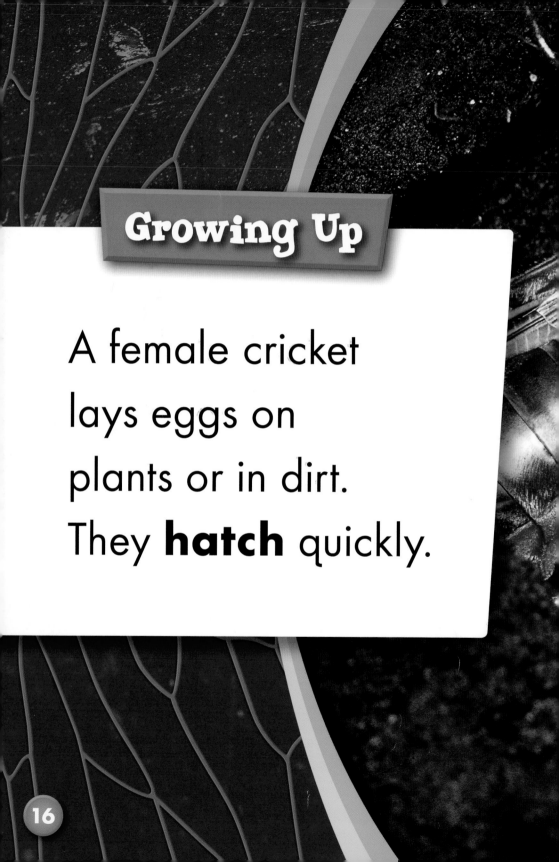

Growing Up

A female cricket
lays eggs on
plants or in dirt.
They **hatch** quickly.

eggs

CRICKET LIFE SPAN:

6 to 8 weeks

Nymphs eat a lot. They **molt** as they grow.

molting

Soon the nymphs grow wings. The new adults are ready to sing!

nymph

Glossary

antennae

feelers connected to the head that sense information around them

molt

to shed skin for growth

eardrums

body parts used for hearing

nymphs

young insects; nymphs look like small adults without full wings.

hatch

to break out of an egg

To Learn More

AT THE LIBRARY

Carle, Eric. *The Very Quiet Cricket*.
New York, N.Y.: Philomel Books, 1990.

Murray, Laura K. *Crickets*. Mankato,
Minn: Creative Education/Creative
Paperbacks, 2016.

Willis, John. *Crickets*. New York, N.Y.:
AV2 by Weigl, 2017.

ON THE WEB

Learning more about crickets
is as easy as 1, 2, 3.

1. Go to www.factsurfer.com.

2. Enter "crickets" into the search box.

3. Click the "Surf" button and you will see a
   list of related web sites.

With factsurfer.com, finding more information
is just a click away.

Index

The images in this book are reproduced through the courtesy of: Old Photographer, front cover; Muhammad Naaim, pp. 4-5; Simon Shim, pp. 6-7; Zety Akhzar, pp. 8-9; Martin Pelanek, pp. 10-11; encikAn, pp. 12-13; up close with nature/ Getty Images, pp. 14-15; Volkova, p. 15; blickwinkel/ Hecker/ Alamy, pp. 16-17; Noppadon stocker, pp. 18-19, 22 (molt); Liew Weng Keong, pp. 20-21, 22 (nymph); Marek R. Swadzba, p. 22 (antennae, eardrum); D. Kucharski K. Kucharska, p. 22 (hatch).